WORLD WAR I

Remembering the Great War

WORLD WAR I
1917–1918
The Turning of the Tide

ROBERT WALKER

Crabtree Publishing Company
www.crabtreebooks.com

WORLD WAR I

Remembering
the Great War

Author: Robert Walker
Editor: Lynn Peppas
Proofreaders: Lisa Slone, Wendy Scavuzzo
Editorial director: Kathy Middleton
Production coordinator: Shivi Sharma
Design concept: Margaret Amy Salter
Cover design: Ken Wright
Photo research: Nivisha Sinha, Crystal Sikkens
Maps: Contentra Technologies
**Production coordinator and
    Prepress technician:** Margaret Amy Salter
Print coordinator: Katherine Berti

Written, developed, and produced by
    Contentra Technologies

Cover: A French Air Force fighter plane takes
    down a German plane
Title page: British troops and tanks advance on
    the Western Front in France, 1918
Contents page: German prisoners of war
    captured during the Battle of Amiens
    arrive at a detention center in France

Photo Credits:
Alamy: 9 (Chronicle), 11 (© akg-images), 12 (© MARKA), 15 (Chronicle), 16 (©
    DIZ Muenchen GmbH, Sueddeutsche Zeitung Photo), 21 (© The Art
    Archive), 24 (© Image Asset Management Ltd.), 25 (© akg-images), 26 (©
    GL Archive), 30 (Chronicle), 33t (© Glasshouse Images)
The Bridgeman Art Library: 29 (Shooting down a Zeppelin during the First
    World War, Hardy, Wilf (Wilfred) (20th century) / Private Collection / ©
    Look and Learn), 35 (Britannic and Mauretania in Ocean Dock,
    Southampton, World War I, 1986 (oil on canvas), Crossley, Harley (1938-
    2013) (Contemporary Artist) / Private Collection), 44 (A French military
    cemetery, Verdun, September 1916 (autochrome), Gervais-Courtellemont,
    Jules (1863-1931) / © Galerie Bilderwelt)
Corbis: 20
FirstWorldWar.com: 14
Getty Images: 5 (Heritage Images), 8 (Print Collector), 23 (Print Collector), 34
    (Archive Photos), 37 (De Agostini)
© Imperial War Museums (INS 6062): 7, 17, 27, 31
India Picture: Content Page (Mary Evans/Robert Hunt Collection/Imperial War
    Museum), 33b ((c)Robert Hunt Library/Mary Evans), 38 (Mary
    Evans/Robert Hunt Collection/Imperial War Museum), 41 ((c) Imperial
    War Museum/Robert Hunt Library/Mary Evans)
Library of Congress: 6 (LC-DIG-hec-04921), 42 (LC-DIG-ppmsca-07634)
Cover: SuperStock
Title: © Hulton-Deutsch Collection/CORBIS
Back covers: Wikimedia Commons: Library and Archives Canada
    (background), Shutterstock: I. Pilon (medals), Shuttertock: IanC66 (airplane)

t=Top, b=Bottom, l=Left, r=Right

Library and Archives Canada Cataloguing in Publication

Walker, Robert, 1980-, author
    World War I : 1917-1918 : the turning of the tide / Robert Walker.

(World War I : remembering the Great War)
Includes index.
Issued in print and electronic formats.
ISBN 978-0-7787-0326-6 (bound).--ISBN 978-0-7787-0391-4 (pbk.).--
ISBN 978-1-4271-7503-8 (pdf).--ISBN 978-1-4271-7497-0 (html)

    1. World War, 1914-1918--Campaigns--Western Front--Juvenile
literature. 2. World War, 1914-1918--United States--Juvenile literature.
3. World War, 1914-1918--Russia--Juvenile literature. I. Title. II. Title:
World War One. III. Title: World War 1. IV. Title: Turning of the tide.

D522.7.W35 2014   j940.3   C2014-903258-7
                                         C2014-903259-5

Library of Congress Cataloging-in-Publication Data

Walker, Robert, 1980-
    World War I, 1917-1918 : the turning of the tide / Robert Walker.
        pages cm. -- (World War I: remembering the Great War)
    Includes index.
    ISBN 978-0-7787-0326-6 (reinforced library binding : alk. paper) --
    ISBN 978-0-7787-0391-4 (pbk. : alk. paper) -- ISBN 978-1-4271-7503-8
    (electronic pdf) -- ISBN 978-1-4271-7497-0 (electronic html)
    1. World War, 1914-1918--Juvenile literature. I. Title.

    D522.7.W35 2014
    940.4'3--dc23

                                    2014017858

Crabtree Publishing Company

www.crabtreebooks.com   1-800-387-7650

Printed in Canada/052014/MA20140505

Published in Canada
Crabtree Publishing
616 Welland Ave.
St. Catharines, Ontario
L2M 5V6

Published in the United States
Crabtree Publishing
PMB 59051
350 Fifth Avenue, 59th Floor
New York, New York 10118

Published in the United Kingdom
Crabtree Publishing
Maritime House
Basin Road North, Hove
BN41 1WR

Published in Australia
Crabtree Publishing
3 Charles Street
Coburg North
VIC, 3058

CONTENTS

THE WAR MARCHES ON

As the Great War dragged into its third year, no end appeared in sight. Both sides, the Allies and Central Powers, were stretched to their limits. Soldiers were exhausted, and resources were strained at home and on the war fronts. Nothing had happened the way either side had expected. Germany and the other Central Powers—Austria-Hungary, the Ottoman Empire, and Bulgaria—had expected an easy victory over the Allies, but it did not happen. In 1916, two major battles, the Battle of Verdun and the Battle of the Somme, ended in catastrophe. Over one million soldiers had died, but neither side was closer to winning the war.

On the Allied side, Russia had been counting on its large army. Germany had great economic and industrial advantages, though. Russia had problems at home, as well. A loss of faith in leadership set the stage for two revolutions. Britain had its own troubles on the battlefield. The Central Powers' strong defenses, poison gases, and better equipment made it difficult for British forces to gain ground. Britain also had political problems at home, with the majority of its people calling for an end to fighting.

But all was not lost for the Allied Forces. The Canadian Corps quickly earned a reputation for getting things done. It helped the Allies gain hard-fought victories. The Allies also looked forward to the arrival of American tanks and soldiers. The added troops and supplies would help the Allies turn the tide. As the stage was set for the closing days of the war, the world waited to see which side would win. Yet no matter who won, the world would change forever.

CHAPTER 1

WAR ON THE EASTERN FRONT

TROUBLES IN RUSSIA

Czar Nicholas II had faced the threat of revolution after losing the Russo-Japanese War in 1905. Many Russians were unhappy. The continuing war was causing severe damage to the economy, and many Russians lost great fortunes. Nicholas II used his power as czar several times to dissolve the **Duma**, the Russian parliament, whenever its members disagreed with his actions. Government corruption was rampant. Food and supplies were scarce, and discontent with the war and the government was widespread.

Russia was no match for the industrially advanced Germany. Russia's large number of soldiers could not make up for the fact that they were unprepared, poorly equipped, and had poor quality **artillery**. There was a great need for changes in the military. Such essential changes were considered by many to be revolutionary; they couldn't be made without great political changes. For Nicholas II, such changes meant giving up absolute authority.

The February Revolution

On March 8, 1917, large groups of strikers clashed with police. Nearly 90,000 people in Petrograd protested against the government. The people faced desperate food shortages. By March 10, strike fever had spread to disgruntled workers. Mobs of protesters grew. They began attacking buildings like police stations.

Major Events

1917

March 15
Czar Nicholas II abdicates.

July 1–6
Kerensky Offensive

Sept 6
Riga Offensive begins.

November 6–7
Bolsheviks take control of the government.

November 26
Russia seeks an armistice with Germany.

1918

March 3
Treaty of Brest-Litovsk

BELOW: *Food shortages plagued the Russian troops as well as the people.*

On March 11, the czar called Russian troops to break up the protests. Their actions sparked violence, with soldiers firing on protesters. But it took only a short time before the soldiers in Petrograd began to side with the strikers. Once again, Nicholas II removed the Duma. But, his plan did not work. Finally, the czar's government stepped down under the pressure of the people. The Duma secretly formed a new provisional, or temporary, government. Within a few days, Nicholas II stepped down. He was the last czar in Russia.

At that time, Russia used the Julian calendar in which the year is longer. As a result, the events were called the February Revolution, even though they happened in March.

The Bolsheviks The Allies quickly recognized the new government, and the new government still supported the war effort. The revolution had left the Russian army near **mutiny**. Still, the Germans feared the power of democratic and patriotic **sentiment** that the revolution had stirred up. Instead of attacking immediately, they took a different approach.

The Bolshevik Party, unlike the provisional government, was against war. Their leader, Vladimir Lenin, had been forced to move to Switzerland. Lenin was a student of Karl Marx, the founder of **communism**.

NICHOLAS II
(1868–1918)

Nicholas II was born in 1868. He became the czar of Russia when his father died in 1894. His views and actions clashed with those of his people and their elected government. He was murdered by revolutionaries in 1918.

The Germans thought that the Bolsheviks might create further divisions in Russia and weaken the war effort. They made a deal with Lenin, allowing him to travel from Switzerland back to Russia. When he arrived, he immediately began calling for Russia to withdraw from the war and for all the land in Russia to be given out to all the people equally. The Bolsheviks quickly gained support, especially among Russian soldiers who just wanted to get home alive.

Kerensky Offensive

The Duma had appointed Aleksandr Fyodorovich Kerensky vice chairman of the Petrograd Soviet of Workers' and Soldiers' Deputies, as well as minister of justice. He became popular and promised the Russian people freedoms in speech, the press, the right to meet, religion, universal **suffrage**, and women's rights. In May 1917, Kerensky was promoted to minister of war and the navy. Soon he was planning a new offensive and visited the war front to encourage the soldiers with inspiring speeches.

Unfortunately, Kerensky could not make up for the weariness of the troops and lack of discipline in the Russian military. On July 1, 1917, the Russian army attacked Austro-Hungarian and German forces in Galicia. The effort initially seemed to be going well, but soon Russian soldiers refused to leave the trenches. By July 6, it was clear that the battle was over for the Russians. It had been a disaster. Two days later, the Austrians and Germans began their **counterattack** and moved through Galicia and into Ukraine with almost no resistance. Kerensky's offensive, also known as the June Offensive, would be Russia's last offensive action in World War I.

The Kerensky Offensive

━━━ Russian front, Jan. 1

0   100 miles
0   200 km

→ Russian advance beginning July 1

••••• Russian retreat by Aug. 3

→ German counterattack

ABOVE: *Russian soldiers flee the battlefield in the Galicia region.*

Riga Offensive

War raged on at the front. By September, Germany had defeated Russian armies in the south. German General Oskar von Hutier turned his sights to the Baltic seaport of Riga and the Russian 12th Army. The German army's approach was fast, intense, and different from the more common strategies. Hutier combined heavy **bombardment** with quick advance of infantry, or foot soldiers. The artillery fire focused at the enemy's rear **lines** to keep reinforcements, or replacement troops, from reaching the front lines. Any troop movement from the rear was met with smoke and poison gas. Hutier used a lightly equipped, fast-moving infantry, called "shock troops." These units struck at weak points along enemy lines. This helped keep the German army from getting stuck. Artillery support focused on the advancing infantry instead of on enemy artillery. The German troops quickly crushed the Russian 12th Army. Russia was in a desperate position. It could not keep fighting much longer.

RED OCTOBER

While the imperial government was gone, the new provisional government still lacked solutions to Russia's problems. Despite strong opposition from the people, the provisional government wanted to stay in the war. Industrial production in 1917 had fallen almost 36 percent from the year before, resulting in mass unemployment. Workers who did have jobs saw their wages fall.

ABOVE: *Vladimir Lenin was a major leader in the Bolshevik Revolution in Russia in 1917. Here, he is urging the deputies of Parliament to give power to his party, the Bolsheviks.*

Among the Russian troops, too, problems had continued to grow. In a sign of revolt in Petrograd and other cities, military garrisons voted not to recognize the provisional government's right to power. Demonstrations began in the larger Russian cities. Almost a half million **civilians** and soldiers protested in Petrograd. The provisional government put down the protest. This fueled the protesters' anger even more. Russian protesters wanted the Bolshevik government to replace the provisional government. Bolshevik leader Vladimir Lenin wanted to take over, so he encouraged the protesters. First, the rebels took control of communication services, bridges, train stations, and a bank. Many takeovers saw no bloodshed. The revolutionaries' final destination was the Winter Palace. It was the former home of the czar and the new headquarters of the provisional government. The revolutionaries arrested many of the provisional government's ministers. The Bolshevik takeover was complete.

This period of revolution is often referred to as Red October, because red was the symbolic color of the Bolsheviks. The workers' militias, or civilian military forces, that helped the revolution in Petrograd were known as the Red Guard. The group would later become the Bolsheviks' Red Army in Russia's civil war of 1918.

On March 3, 1918, Russia signed a peace treaty with the Central Powers in the city of Brest-Litovsk. Russia was no longer in the war. This meant the Central Powers could move troops from the Eastern Front to the Western Front. The treaty dealt a blow to Russia. The country lost to the Central Powers 32 percent of its farmable land, 69 percent of its industry, a third of the nation's population, and huge stores of natural resources. Lenin felt he had been wronged by the terms of this treaty and hoped that one day he might make up for it by spreading his revolution across the world.

ABOVE: *The German foreign secretary signs the Treaty of Brest-Litovsk, marking Russia's withdrawal from the war.*

WHAT DO YOU THINK?
How did Russia's surrender affect the war?

CHAPTER 2

ITALIAN AND OTHER FRONTS

Major Events

1915

May 23
Italy joins the war.

1917

August 19
Eleventh Battle of Isonzo

October 15
Battle of Mahiwa

October 24
Battle of Caporetto

1918

September 15
Battle of Vardar

October 30
Ottomans sign Treaty of Mudros

November 1
Serbian army retakes Belgrade

Fighting in World War I took place on many different fronts. These fronts often protected important natural resources, colonies, and supply routes. Fighting on these fronts would draw troops and resources away from the Western and Eastern Fronts.

ITALIAN BATTLES

The Italian army was considered to be one of the larger Allied armies. It had almost 875,000 men when Italy entered the war. However, these soldiers were poorly equipped, lacking **reserves** of artillery, ammunition, and transportation. Even worse, they lacked leadership. Luigi Cadorna was appointed chief of staff in 1914.

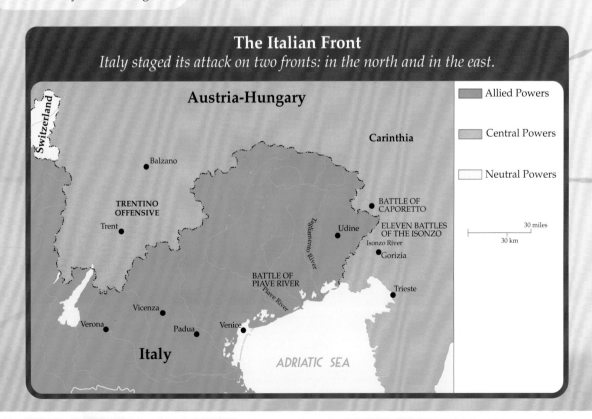

The Italian Front
Italy staged its attack on two fronts: in the north and in the east.

Austria-Hungary

Carinthia

Switzerland

Balzano

TRENTINO OFFENSIVE

Trent

Tagliamento River

Udine

BATTLE OF CAPORETTO

ELEVEN BATTLES OF THE ISONZO

Isonzo River

Gorizia

BATTLE OF PIAVE RIVER

Piave River

Trieste

Vicenza

Verona

Padua

Venice

Italy

ADRIATIC SEA

Allied Powers

Central Powers

Neutral Powers

30 miles

30 km

Cardona was unpopular with his troops and had difficulty getting necessary equipment. His strategies did not include artillery support. He also became known for his cruelty. More than 750 men were given the death penalty for being cowards, and 217 officers were let go for not doing their job right.

The Battles of Isonzo and Caporetto

Italy joined the war on May 23, 1915, with plans to invade Austria-Hungary. Italy's focus was on the northern Trentino region and along the Isonzo River to the east. The Isonzo was a **boundary** between the mountains of Austria-Hungary and the plains of northern Italy. The First Battle of Isonzo began in June 1915. The fighting there continued on and off over the course of the next two years. It is uncertain exactly how many separate battles took place. Most estimate that there were at least 12.

The Eleventh Battle of Isonzo began on August 19, 1917. Italian troops attacked the Austrian lines north of Gorizia and the hills between Gorizia and Trieste. The northern troops advanced quickly into enemy territory, and the Austro-Hungarian troops were alarmed. Fearing collapse, they requested the Germans come to their aid. The Italian victory didn't last long. The Battle of Caporetto, also known as the Twelfth Battle of Isonzo, began on October 24, 1917. The Germans now supported the Austro-Hungarian forces.

ABOVE: *This painting by Thomas Baumgartner illustrates the fighting on the Italian Front.*

The battle began with vicious artillery **shelling**, gas, and explosives. Using Hutier's tactics, the Austro-Hungarian and German troops soon broke through enemy lines. This beat down Italian troops even more. Many on the front lines surrendered or **retreated**. Making matters worse, Cadorna had sent his reserve troops too far away to enter the fight quickly. By nightfall, Cadorna ordered a retreat to the defensive line of the Tagliamento River.

In a stroke of luck for Italy, Austro-Hungarian forces had advanced so quickly that they were outrunning their supplies. Waiting for supplies delayed troop movement. That limited options for attack. As the Battle of Caporetto was drawing to a close, Austro-Hungarian leaders chose to attack the Italian line at Corino on November 4. The attack proved to be a bloodbath for Cadorna. He ordered another retreat to positions north of Venice and the Piave River. Italian troops had suffered huge casualties. At least 300,000 were dead, wounded, taken prisoner, or **deserted**. This battle marked Cadorna's final retreat. General Armando Diaz promptly took command. He would try to help Italy recover from its setbacks.

**ARMANDO DIAZ
(1861–1928)**

Armando Diaz went to the military schools of Naples and Turin. He served under Luigi Cadorna leading up to the war, and they reorganized the Italian army. Diaz continued to serve under Cadorna when the war began. He replaced Cadorna after the Italian defeat at Caporetto.

The Battle of the Piave River

With new reinforcements, the Italians were able to hold the Piave line. Neither side was able to gain much ground. By spring 1918, the Germans pulled their troops off the Italian Front. This left Austria-Hungary to fight alone. The Austro-Hungarians were also having problems in their upper ranks. Two commanders, Count Franz Conrad von Hötzendorf and General Svetozar Borojević von Bojna, were arguing about who would lead the next attack. It was finally decided that each general would lead part of the army. The decision turned out to be unwise. The armies were weaker when separate.

The Battle of the Piave River marked the last major military offensive for Austria-Hungary. The defeat also paved the way to the end of the Austro-Hungarian Empire. For the Italians, the battle was a landmark; a popular saying of the time was that either the Italians would be heroes and hold the Piave, or they should all be killed.

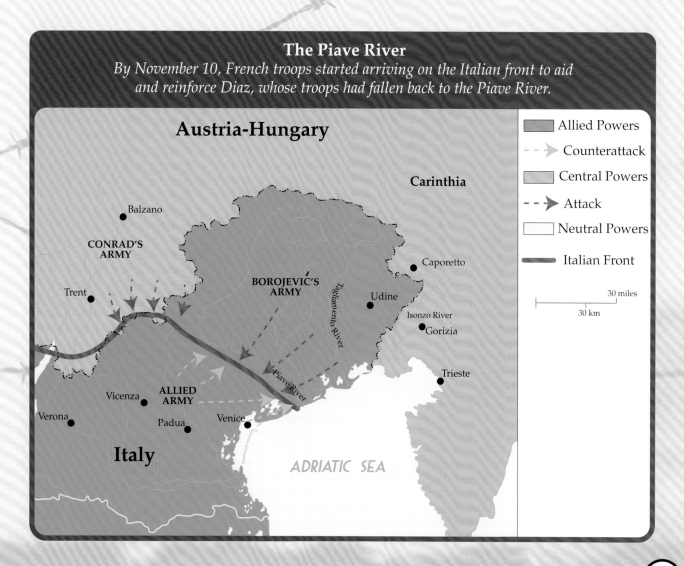

The Piave River

By November 10, French troops started arriving on the Italian front to aid and reinforce Diaz, whose troops had fallen back to the Piave River.

Austria-Hungary

Carinthia

CONRAD'S ARMY

Balzano

Trent

BOROJEVIĆ'S ARMY

Caporetto

Udine

Isonzo River

Gorizia

Tagliamento River

Trieste

ALLIED ARMY

Vicenza

Piave River

Verona

Padua

Venice

Italy

ADRIATIC SEA

	Allied Powers
	Counterattack
	Central Powers
	Attack
	Neutral Powers
	Italian Front

30 miles

30 km

Also, communication was difficult between the two groups in the mountainous region. Conrad went after the city of Verona, while Borojević marched on Padua. The offensive ended badly for Conrad. General Diaz had received earlier information about the attack. The Italian 5th and 6th armies crushed Conrad's troops.

With Conrad defeated, Diaz then went after the Austrian supply lines with bombers. He called up the Italian 9th Army, which he had kept in reserve. These soldiers stood up to Borojević's forces, forcing them to withdraw on June 22 and June 23. The Allies had now gained the advantage on the Italian Front.

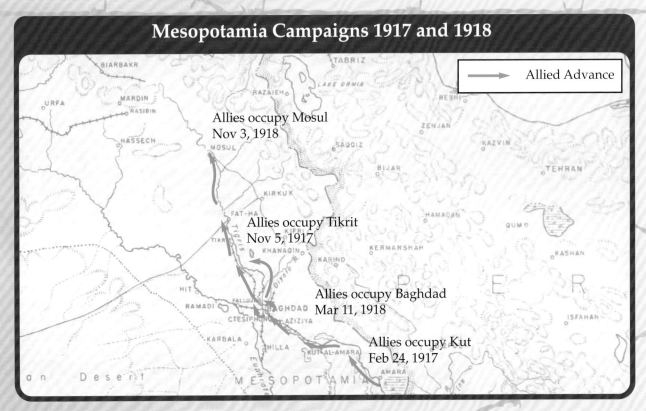

Mesopotamia Campaigns 1917 and 1918

Allied Advance

Allies occupy Mosul
Nov 3, 1918

Allies occupy Tikrit
Nov 5, 1917

Allies occupy Baghdad
Mar 11, 1918

Allies occupy Kut
Feb 24, 1917

WORLD WAR I ON OTHER FRONTS

The major nations of World War I controlled many territories overseas. These territories were important sources of troops and resources. Fighting spread to these locations as well.

War in Mesopotamia

To keep its navy strong, Britain depended on oil from Middle-Eastern areas, such as Mesopotamia—modern day Iraq. When Turkey entered the war in 1914, the British feared they would be cut off from this area, which had long been part of the Turkish Ottoman Empire. Seeking to protect their territories and trade routes, British troops moved into Mesopotamia in 1915.

ABOVE: *Local citizens watched as Allied troops marched through Baghdad with their Turkish prisoners.*

They enjoyed early success but soon met with Turkish and German opposition. **Morale** dropped and supplies dwindled through the winter. The British tried four times to overcome their Turkish opponents, only to suffer 23,000 casualties. On April 29, 1916, the city of Kut fell, and British commander Sir Charles Townshend surrendered. He and at least 10,000 of his remaining troops were taken prisoner. This was the largest single surrender in British history up to that time.

In 1917, Major-General Sir Frederick Stanley Maude took control of the British forces in Mesopotamia. He had learned from the previous failures there. He also had help from new Indian forces. He was able to defeat the Turks and capture Baghdad by March 1917. In the fall of 1918, the Turks wanted out of the war.

They began negotiations with Allied forces. On October 30, 1918, the Ottomans signed the Treaty of Mudros aboard the British battleship *Agamemnon*, ending their involvement in the war.

War in Africa

In February 1916, German Lieutenant Colonel Paul von Lettow-Vorbeck had faced a massive invasion of British and colonial troops in German East Africa, led by South African general Jan Christiaan Smuts. The attack was part of a larger plan, with Belgian forces invading from the west and British forces attacking from the south. Although he was greatly outnumbered, Lettow-Vorbeck used the harsh climate and terrain to his advantage. He used a patient **strategy**, which included letting the tropical diseases do considerable damage to the enemy.

WHAT DO YOU KNOW?

A NATURAL BORN LEADER

Paul von Lettow-Vorbeck started his military career as an artillery officer. After a short service on the German General Staff, he served as an **expeditionary** soldier in China during the Boxer Uprising and in Africa during the Hottentot-Herero Rebellion. In 1914, he was promoted to lieutenant colonel.

Knowing that the Allies eventually would drive his army out of East Africa, Lettow-Vorbeck refused to make a single all-or-nothing stand. He led an invasion of Mozambique in December 1917. By raiding Portuguese garrisons there, he was able to resupply his army. He was able to move forward as far as Quelimane on July 1, 1918. By this time, the war had ended in Europe. Word had not yet reached Lettow-Vorbeck and his forces though. He continued fighting, invading British-held Rhodesia. He took the city of Kasama on November 18, 1918, two days after the war had officially ended. Word finally reached Lettow-Vorbeck, and he opened negotiations with Britain. On November 25, 1918, he surrendered at Abercorn.

BELOW: *Paul von Lettow-Vorbeck*

Even with loss after loss, Britain continued to send more troops and resources to the **battlefront**. Lettow-Vorbeck responded to the Allied advances by slowly giving in to the advancing troops, yet doing as much damage as possible to the Allied soldiers. One tactic involved abruptly turning retreating troops around for an attack before retreating farther. At the Battle of Mahiwa on October 15, 1917, Lettow-Vorbeck went up against British forces that outnumbered his own by four to one. But even with odds against them, Lettow-Vorbeck's troops cost the British forces some 2,700 casualties, while suffering just over 500 among themselves.

The Battle of Vardar

The Battle of Vardar was the final offensive operation in Macedonia. In September 1918, Allied and Central forces met on the Salonika Front in northern Greece. Both sides were almost evenly matched.

The Allied attack was set along a 6 mile (9.6 km) front. Fighting began on September 15 with an artillery bombardment against the positions held by the German 11th and Bulgarian 1st armies. The attack caught the Germans and Bulgarians off guard. With this relatively easy victory, Allied forces advanced rapidly along the front.

BELOW: *British forces captured these Bulgarian soldiers during the Second Battle of Doiran.*

WHAT DO YOU THINK?
How did the fighting on fronts other than the Eastern and Western affect the outcome of the war?

The Serbian 2nd Army then took Mount Vetrenik and Mount Sokol, as well as the low ground near Mount Dobropolje. Allied forces broke through the Central lines on September 17. They reached the Vardar River by September 21 and forced the Bulgarian army into a general retreat. A French cavalry **brigade** attacked the Crna River on September 22. On September 29, the French cavalry entered Skopje after an Allied advance of 57 miles (92 km) in only six days.

At first, Allied attacks around Lake Doiran from September 16–18 failed. But on September 20, the Bulgarian 1st Army began to withdraw. British and Greek forces took the high ground of Pip Ridge and Grande Couronne. The Serbian army continued to advance. On November 1, the Serbs retook their capital, Belgrade. French forces had occupied Bulgaria and entered Romania by November. On November 3, Allied troops took Bar in Montenegro and joined up with the Serbian 2nd Army. The same day, Austria-Hungary signed an **armistice** with the Allies.

The Vardar Offensive

The taking of high positions such as Mounts Vetrenik and Sokol gave the Allies the advantage of higher ground.

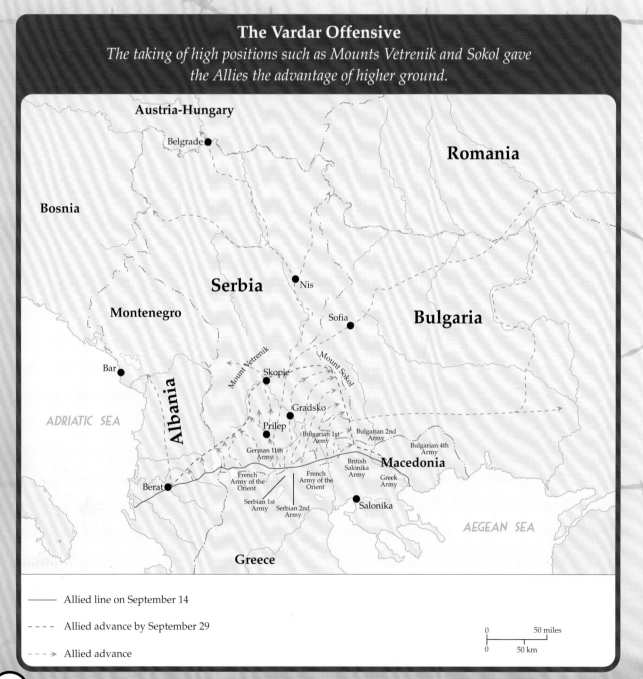

Allied line on September 14

- - - - Allied advance by September 29

- - -→ Allied advance

0   50 miles
0   50 km

CHAPTER 3

WAR ON THE WESTERN FRONT

As the war raged on, Allied forces faced difficult decisions. Perhaps the most important was who would lead. In Britain, Prime Minister H. H. Asquith was replaced in December 1916 by David Lloyd George. In France, a new commander-in-chief, Robert Nivelle, took over. Changes in the British command took place in 1917. The new Allied commanders hoped that new approaches to the war would help bring it to an end.

THE NIVELLE METHOD

Nivelle proposed a strategy he believed could win the war. His method consisted of attacks using a different artillery strategy. Nivelle would order bombardment of Germans lines and then call a halt. He thought this strategy would force the enemy to reveal its artillery positions by returning fire. When the enemy positions were revealed, Nivelle would send in small infantry units directly behind the cover of concentrated fire. The artillery fire would slowly creep into German lines just ahead of the advancing infantry.

The Hindenburg Line

The Hindenburg Line was a major German defensive position, stretching from Arras to Laffaux. In the spring of 1917, the German army decided to pull back to a position it could defend more easily. As they retreated, the

Major Events

1917

April 9–May 16
Arras Offensive

April 29
Mutinies in the French army

June 7
Allies capture Messines Ridge.

July 31–November 6
Third Battle of Ypres

November 20–December 7
Battle of Cambrai

1918

March 21–April 4
Second Battle of the Somme

WHAT DO YOU THINK?
What was the major difference between Nivelle's strategy and earlier strategies?

German forces practiced a **scorched earth** policy, in which they poisoned wells, set booby traps, and destroyed roads and railways. This move shortened the line significantly. Nivelle would soon test his strategy against the Hindenburg Line defenses.

Battle of Arras

Allied bombardments began on March 20, 1917. The British developed a new poison gas that they used during the bombardment. It stopped the German artillery forces. At the northern point of the battlefront, the Canadian Corps was preparing to attack Vimy Ridge. Vimy Ridge was a well-defended section of the German line. Canadian troops had to penetrate three lines of German trenches, tunnels, machine gun **bunkers**, and miles of barbed wire. By the end of the afternoon, Canadian forces controlled most of the ridge. They took over the rest

in the next few days. Both sides suffered huge numbers of casualties.

Nivelle's plan of quick-moving units of soldiers proved less successful when applied to large groups. Coordination was difficult and artillery fire could not break through barbed wire or the German defense. On April 16, Nivelle launched his main attack in Champagne. The attack was unsuccessful. The French troops thought they were firing on occupied German trenches. They soon found themselves in a barren, open area. There, they became easy targets for the Germans. Allied forces lost the element of surprise. French observation planes were shot down. This left German artillery free to target the French tanks. In five days, 120,000 French soldiers were wounded or killed. The losses left French soldiers very discouraged.

BELOW: *British troops follow an officer out of the trenches to charge German lines during the Arras campaign.*

ABOVE: *German prisoners carry a wounded Canadian soldier during the Battle of Vimy Ridge.*

Mutiny in the French Army

French soldiers began to lose faith in their leaders after the Nivelle offensive failed. French troops were exhausted after the disaster in Champagne. On April 29, they rebelled by refusing to move forward. During the first three weeks of May, French soldiers' refusal to attack spread along the battlefront. More and more soldiers failed to do any more than defend their current trenches. The French Army was in a state of mutiny.

In addition to the disaster of the Nivelle offensive, food shortages, lack of proper medical care, and unanswered demands for **leaves** caused unrest among the troops. Yet even with widespread mutinies, Nivelle ordered another attack. On May 15, hoping to end the mutinies, French War Minister Paul Painlevé assigned Philippe Pétain to replace Nivelle. But soldiers still refused to attack. By June, more than 50 French divisions faced mutinies. This left only two fighting divisions between advancing German forces and the city of Paris.

The French leaders kept word of the problem from reaching the other Allied nations. Pétain moved quickly to stop the spread of mutiny. He worked to supply rations, improve medical care, and create a program of rotating leaves. This meant that soldiers would get to spend more time away from the front. Many soldiers suffered harsh punishment for their actions. Some were even tried and executed for mutiny. With the French army concerned with regaining order, British forces would lead most Allied activity during the summer.

The Battle of Messines

The Allies believed that securing the high ground along the Messines-Wytschaete Ridge in Belgium was an important move. Before General Herbert Plumer and his 2nd Army could launch the offensive, British engineers dug six mine shafts under the German front lines. Each tunnel was connected to a chamber loaded with explosives. Preparations and plans for this offensive took nearly 18 months.

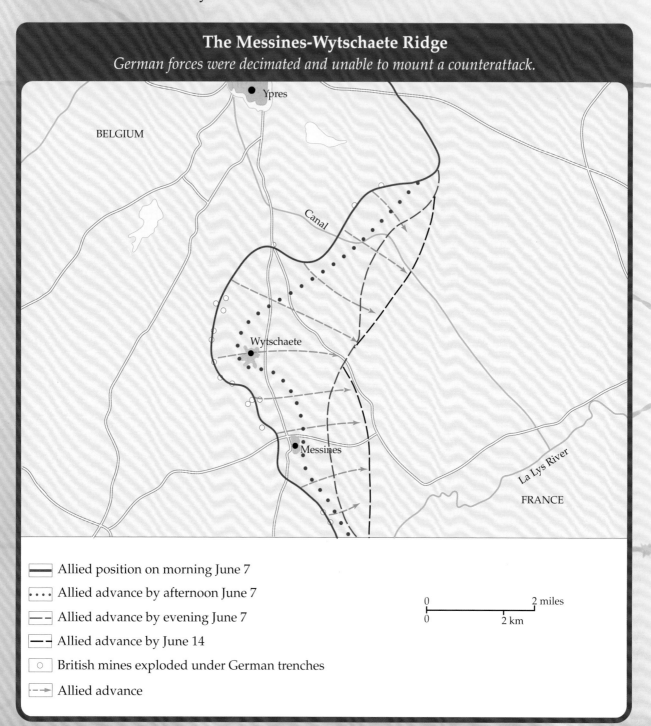

The Messines-Wytschaete Ridge
German forces were decimated and unable to mount a counterattack.

Ypres

BELGIUM

Canal

Wytschaete

Messines

La Lys River

FRANCE

— Allied position on morning June 7

···· Allied advance by afternoon June 7

--- Allied advance by evening June 7

— — Allied advance by June 14

○ British mines exploded under German trenches

---→ Allied advance

0   2 miles

0   2 km

The attack began with heavy bombardment of enemy lines. For 17 days, British troops fought to crush enemy artillery. On June 7, 1917, the British began a significant artillery bombardment then stopped. They hoped this would draw the Germans out in anticipation of an attack. Then the British detonated about 500 tons (454 tonnes) of explosives stored underground. The blast was so massive and earsplitting that it was heard as far away as London. Almost 10,000 German soldiers were killed, and some were buried alive. Immediately following the blast, Plumer ordered an artillery attack of smoke and poison gas shells. By the time British troops charged over the top, they had crushed the German forces. As British tanks rolled over the trench lines, firing off more poisonous gas shells, the remaining German troops had no choice but to abandon the ridge.

WHAT DO YOU THINK?
Do you think the French commanders handled the mutinies well? If you were in command, how would you deal with the situation?

ABOVE: *These Australian soldiers are studying a model showing the German trenches and no man's land the day before the Battle of Messines.*

The Battle of Hill 70

The fighting at Passchendaele had become intense. General Douglas Haig asked for attacks to be made at other locations. He hoped that other attacks would take the German focus away from Passchendaele. The Canadian Corps planned to attack the French city of Lens in August 1917. The Germans occupied Lens. The Canadian Corps decided it would be better to capture the high ground near Lens, which was called Hill 70.

If the Canadians could attack and control this hill, German forces would be stretched further. They would have to counterattack. The Canadian forces captured many of their objectives during the Battle of Hill 70. They defended their position against 21 unsuccessful German counterattacks. The Canadians lost more than 9,000 soldiers during the fight for Hill 70. They succeeded in killing or wounding at least 20,000 German soldiers. The city of Lens was never taken. Still, the attack on Hill 70 had a significant impact on the German position.

BELOW: *During the Third Battle of Ypres, the horrible, muddy conditions in no man's land discouraged many French soldiers.*

Third Battle of Ypres: Passchendaele

The success at Messines encouraged the Allies to stage a third attack at Passchendaele. British and Canadian troops were chosen for the assault. However, Allied forces faced numerous problems. The demoralized French forces continued their mutinies. And the British High Command refused to send extra reinforcements for the mission. The offensive took a long time to plan as well. During that time, the Allies lost the momentum they had gained at Messines.

When the offensive began on July 31, 1917, Allied forces attacked with the largest artillery preparation of the war.

Unfortunately, the bombing targeted the area to be covered by advancing Allied troops. The bombed terrain and bad weather at the time made troop movement extremely difficult. Led by General Hubert de la Poer Gough, Allied troops did their best to slog through wet, muddy no-man's land. They were told the Allied **intelligence** reports said that the Germans would not be strong enough to defend their position. They also were told that a major Allied victory would cause German forces to collapse. The intelligence proved disastrously wrong. Well-prepared German troops were on the alert.

German fighter planes and machine gun fire slaughtered Allied troops, who were bogged down in the mud. In addition, the new German poison, mustard gas, clouded the battlefield. It caused severe burns to the skin, eyes, and lungs. Despite these hardships and obstacles, Canadian, French, and British troops took Passchendaele Ridge as well as the village of Passchendaele by November 6.

Overall, Allied gains at Passchendaele were limited. Those gains came at great cost.

Cambrai

The Allies felt they badly needed a solid victory after Passchendaele. Allied commanders decided to push on to Cambrai, France. Allied forces were lead by General J. H. G. Byng. The offensive used large numbers of tanks in the war for the first time. Byng decided against an initial artillery bombing. Paired with the good terrain, the strategy allowed for the element of surprise.

RIGHT: *In the Battle of Cambrai, British forces saw success at first. Here, British machine gunners have occupied a German trench.*

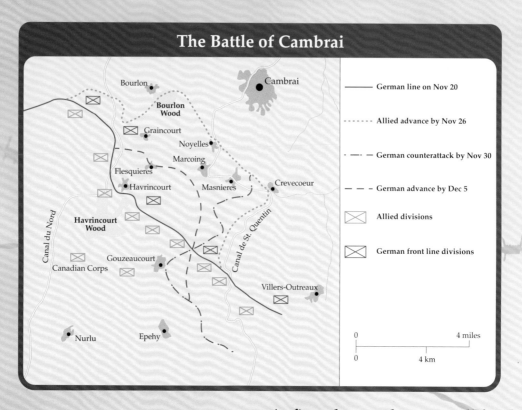

The Battle of Cambrai

———	German line on Nov 20
·········	Allied advance by Nov 26
—·—·—	German counterattack by Nov 30
— — —	German advance by Dec 5
⊠	Allied divisions
⊠	German front line divisions

Bourlon
Cambrai
Bourlon Wood
Graincourt
Noyelles
Marcoing
Flesquieres
Havrincourt
Masnieres
Crevecoeur
Canal du Nord
Havrincourt Wood
Canal de St. Quentin
Gouzeaucourt
Canadian Corps
Villers-Outreaux
Nurlu
Epehy

0   4 miles
0   4 km

ABOVE: *Allied tank losses at Cambrai were high. This Mark IV tank got stuck trying to cross a German trench.*

At first, the attack went well for the Allies. They were able to punch a 5-mile (8 km) **breach** into the Hindenburg Line. Byng was ready to take advantage of this with cavalry, as well as with infantry. However, the Allies' good fortune didn't last long. After penetrating enemy lines, the tanks began to break down in large numbers. German reinforcements had time to plug the gap that the Allied forces had made. The British cavalry and infantry were unable to maintain the breach and partially withdrew on December 3. Both sides lost approximately 45,000 men, including 11,000 German and 9,000 British prisoners. Neither side permanently gained any ground.

Mobile Warfare In the later years of the war, the use of tanks began to shake up the nature of trench warfare. Tanks could roll over the barbed wire

LEFT: *German troops advanced toward the Western Front for the Second Battle of the Somme. Horses transported their supplies.*

leading up to trench systems. Their heavy armor protected them from infantry fire. At Cambrai, the British equipped their tanks with fascines—large bundles of sticks that could be dropped in the trenches to allow the tanks to cross. Once the heavy tanks had crossed the trenches, they created a breach in the enemy lines. Then the lighter tanks and infantry came in behind to clear the trenches.

Early tanks had their limitations. It was easy for them to get stuck while crossing trenches. The British Whippet, one of the fastest tanks, ran at a relatively speedy 8.3 mph (13.4 kph). Lack of speed often made it difficult for tanks to take advantage of breakthroughs. Limited visibility and overheating were issues for these early tanks, as well. Many did not have good radios either, limiting communication in the middle of battle. At Cambrai, tank losses were heavy. By November 23, only 92 out of 474 tanks were still operational.

Second Battle of the Somme

After Russia withdrew from the war, the Germans were able to move more troops to the Western Front in the spring of 1918. Code-named "St. Michael," the offensive at the Somme River began on March 21, 1918, under the leadership of General Erich Ludendorff. German forces would attack the Allied positions along a 60-mile (97 km) front from Arras to La Fère in northern France.

The battle began with intense artillery bombardments. Central Power forces were able to drive back the British 5th Army. The Central Powers thought that the French forces would remain near Paris. Although French forces did arrive to help the British, French commanders failed to communicate and work together. Their poor performance led to Ferdinand Foch's appointment as commander-in-chief of the Allied forces in France.

CHAPTER 4

WAR BY AIR AND BY SEA

WAR IN THE AIR

World War I would bring many changes in air and sea warfare. Among the most significant developments were those that happened in the air. When World War I broke out in 1914, powered flight was barely over 10 years old. Although some aircraft had been used in the Italian-Turkish War of 1911, most flying was done by civilians. Leaders used the first planes in wartime for reconnaissance—observing enemy lines or helping direct artillery fire. Planes needed to be as light as possible to get off the ground. This left no room for bombs or guns. As air reconnaissance came into wider use, both sides started to come up with ways to shoot down each other's planes. Early airplanes were made of cloth and wood, making them quite fragile. It took little more than machine-gun fire to bring down a plane.

Flying Blimps

Zeppelins were large, slow-moving **aerials**. They caused quite a commotion when they first flew over Britain. Flight in general was still a new concept. Zeppelins had the potential for massive destruction if used as bombers. They were difficult to steer, and the hydrogen gas that filled the balloon was extremely **combustible**. However, their greatest advantage was their ability to fly higher than planes. This made them difficult to shoot down. They could also carry many more bombs than planes could. Although they played only a small role in the war, they were ideal for strategic bombardments. They were used to attack military and civilian targets.

The first German airship raid on London took place on May 31, 1915. A second attack took place on September 15. By the end of the war, British cities had suffered 51 airship attacks. More than 4,000 pounds (1.814 kg) of explosives were dropped and 557 lives were lost. By 1917, however, German and British airships were used mostly for reconnaissance. Newly designed planes could fly higher, and incendiary bullets—or bullets designed to start fires—could cause the hydrogen-filled aircraft to explode.

ABOVE: *One of the weaknesses of zeppelins was that they could easily catch on fire when attacked by enemy aircraft.*

ABOVE: *The Vickers F. B.5 biplane was also known as a Gunbus.*

Fighter Planes

At first, pilots used pistols for shooting. They steered the plane with one hand and fired the pistol with the other. In a two-seater plane, the pilot could focus on flying while the passenger used a rifle or shotgun to fire at the enemy. Propellers on standard aircraft at the time were mounted at the front of the plane. However, in 1913, Britain developed a plane with the propeller mounted behind the engine. The passenger would sit in front of the pilot and operate a machine gun. The Vickers F.B.5 Gunbus, based on an improvement of this design, became the first mass-produced plane made for air combat.

Despite the convenience of the seating, the Vickers could not perform as well as a plane with the propeller at the front in terms of speed, control, and overall handling. But placing the propeller in front of the machine gun caused a problem: How could the pilot fire without hitting the propeller? German designer Franz Schneider solved the problem with an **interrupter** mechanism. It **synchronized** the firing of the machine gun and the rotation of the propeller. This allowed for bullets to pass safely between the spinning blades. However, the German military showed little interest in the device.

French engineer Raymond Saulnier tried his hand unsuccessfully with the interrupter device. Instead, he thought to attach steel plates to the propeller to protect against the bullets. But the steel plates did not work either. Then, Dutch aircraft manufacturer Anthony Fokker came into the picture. He designed and built the first practical synchronized machine gun mounted in the body of the airplane. This invention marked the beginnings of the single-man fighter plane.

Sky Bombers

Even with the modest success of airships as bombers, the Allied and Central Powers were both developing airplanes to do the job. The first bomber plane was the French Voisin. It was a single-engine plane that could reach the impressive speed of 85 mph (137 kph) and carry over 600 pounds (272 kg) of explosives.

BELOW: *A Handley Page bomber*

The Russians also designed and built their own line of bomber planes, called Ilya Muromets. First built in 1913, the planes had a 100-foot (30.5 m) **wingspan** and could carry a crew of five men. Mounted with machine guns, the Ilya Muromet could fly as high as 9,000 feet (2,743 m). It had a top speed of more than 80 mph (129 kph) and could carry a bomb load of almost 1,500 pounds (680 kg). The Ilya Muromets were among the most successful bombers in World War I. They flew more than 400 missions with very few casualties.

The Italians also built a bomber, called the Caproni. It could fly at more than 90 mph (145 kph) and carry almost 1,200 pounds (544 kg) of bombs. Yet it was Great Britain that built more bombers than any other country in the war. The first was the Handley Page bomber that appeared in 1916. The plane could carry almost 1,800 pounds (817 kg) of bombs and fly at 90 mph (145 kph). In 1917, a newer model had top speeds of over 97 mph (156 kph).

Germany used two strategic bombers later in the war: the Friedrichshafen and the Gotha. Each plane had twin engines, could carry 1,000 pounds (454 kg) of bombs, and reached a speed of 87 mph (140 kph). The Gotha was particularly effective in destroying supply depots.

Flying Aces

The term *flying aces* was first used in French newspapers to distinguish any pilot who took down five enemy planes. Of all the pilots who achieved this status in World War I, one of the most accomplished was Canadian Billy Bishop.

> "The development of air power in its broadest sense, and including the development of all means of combating missiles that travel through the air, whether fired or dropped, is the first essential to our survival in war."
>
> VISCOUNT HUGH M. TRENCHARD, MARSHAL OF THE BRITISH ROYAL AIR FORCE

WHAT DO YOU THINK?
How did the uses of airplanes change over the course of the war?

ABOVE: *Canadian pilot Arthur Roy Brown is said to have brought down the feared German ace called the "Red Baron" in 1918.*

Flying for England, he was the British Empire's top-scoring fighter pilot. He began the war as part of the Canadian Expeditionary Force, serving as a soldier for his first year. In 1915, he requested transfer to Britain's Royal Flying Corps to train to be a pilot. Bishop earned his pilot's wings in 1917, and soon after he was sent to France to fight. He quickly earned a reputation for downing enemy planes. In fact, in his first year, Bishop received the Victoria Cross—Britain's highest war honor—for flying behind enemy lines and downing three German planes.

RIGHT: *By the end of 1917, fighter pilot Billy Bishop had shot down 47 planes. He added another 25 in 1918.*

33

ABOVE: *When the war broke out, German U-boats had standing orders to sink any enemy craft without warning.*

War at Sea

Britain is an island nation. Its geography protects it from enemy invasion. But being cut off from the rest of the world means dependence on imports. This in turn means needing a large commercial fleet and strong navy to protect it. At the beginning of the war, Britain had 29 ships in service, with 13 under construction. Germany, on the other hand, had 18 ships, with 9 under construction. Neither nation wanted to go head-to-head before all of their ships were ready for service. When the war started, Britain used its navy to protect important trade routes and to prevent supply ships from reaching Germany. Germany used its navy to lay mines in enemy harbors and to attack British merchant ships. Most of the fighting at sea took place under the water. German submarines, or **U-boats**, waged war against Allied merchant ships.

Fighting Underwater

By early the 1900s, four developments made a combat submarine possible: a watertight steel hull, electric motors, battery power, and the self-propelled **torpedo**. All modern submarines carried torpedoes and, for fighting above the water, medium-sized guns mounted on the submarine's deck. **Periscopes** allowed for viewing the surface of the water while the submarine was still submerged. Torpedo attacks could be made from more than 10,000 yards (9,144 m) away. However, to fire torpedoes, submarines had to rise to the surface.

During the early years of the war, submarines enjoyed relative safety under water. Enemy ships could not see them down there. The hydrophone—an underwater listening device that British engineers developed and installed on Royal Navy vessels—ended this security. Another threat to submarines was the invention of the depth charge, a bomb that would explode once it reached a certain depth. Water mines also endangered submarines. In fact, Britain and the United States had mine lines running across the exits from the Baltic Sea to the North Sea. By the war's end, German submarines had sunk 5,554 Allied and merchant ships, as well as many warships. The German navy had suffered serious losses as well. Allied forces had destroyed 178 of Germany's 371 submarines.

WHAT DO YOU KNOW?

PROTECTIVE PAINT
Camouflage paint on the hull of a merchant ship helped protect it from German U-boats. The strange designs made it hard for the U-boats to determine the ship's course and aim torpedoes at it.

BELOW: *The* Britannic *on the left and the* Mauretania *on the right were British ships used as hospital ships. The* Mauretania *was also used to carry troops and was camouflaged to make it hard for the Germans to see.*

35

THE END OF THE WAR

As the war raged on through 1918, Germany's allies increasingly struggled against the Allied advances. Food and supplies became scarce. They faced starvation, disease, unrest, and military desertions.

Bulgaria achieved most of its goals in the war early, capturing territory from Serbia and Romania. After gaining little in the Treaty of Brest-Litovsk (see page 9), Bulgaria began to doubt it would be well rewarded even if Germany won.

The Ottoman Empire was poor and had lower industrial development. The Ottomans suffered heavily from the **attrition** of the war. Food shortages and outbreaks of diseases like typhus, malaria, and smallpox wore Turkey down. Military demands drained the economy. Heavy casualties and mass desertions left the Turkish army at only about one sixth of its full strength in 1918.

As Austria-Hungary experienced shortages and defeats, Socialist support began to spread. Political unrest grew among Austria-Hungary's numerous minority populations. Bosnians, Czechs, Slovaks, and many other people in the Austro-Hungarian empire did not want to be ruled by Austria and Hungary any more. The desire for independence began pulling the empire apart even further.

The war stretched the ties between the Central Powers over time. As its allies struggled, Germany had to send more and more supplies and troops to help. German support often came with Germany demanding greater control over its allies. Many began to resent Germany's strength and dominance.

ABOVE: *A British Mark I tank smashes through a German trench to victory at the Battle of Cambrai.*

As 1918 continued, Germany was left more and more to carry the load of war by itself.

THE AMIENS OFFENSIVE

The Battle of Amiens was the beginning of the end for the German armies. A well-trained and well-armed Allied force, led by Canadian and Australian troops, broke the German lines on August 8, 1918. The Germans were pushed back several miles to the Hindenburg Line (see page 19).

Following unsuccessful German offensives in the spring of 1918, the Allies called for a regroup and counterattacked on the Western Front. Preparations for this movement were made in secret. They included a large **counterintelligence** operation to trick German forces about the real location of Allied troops. This attack proved one of the most successful of the war.

At the beginning of the attack, the Canadian Corps moved 8 miles (12.8 km) through the German defenses. That was the most successful day of combat for the Allies on the Western Front up to that point. In response, Germany rushed reinforcements to the battlefield to prevent a breakthrough. Continuing to fight was becoming far more difficult and costly. The attacking forces were moving beyond the range of German guns. By the beginning of August 11, most German offensive operations had ground to a halt.

ABOVE: *German prisoners of war captured during the Battle of Amiens were forced to march to a detention center on the Western Front.*

The Saint-Mihiel Salient

The American Expeditionary Force (AEF) had provided support to the French forces at Belleau Wood and in the second battle for the Marne. American commander General John J. Pershing and Allied Supreme Commander Ferdinand Foch decided that the 1st Army of the AEF would establish its headquarters in the Saint-Mihiel **salient**. The salient had been under German occupation since the fall of 1914. By heavily fortifying the area, Germany effectively had blocked all rail transport between Paris and the Eastern Front. This had made it harder for the Allies to move troops and supplies between the fronts.

Fighting began on September 12, 1918, with the push of Allied tanks across the trenches at Saint-Mihiel. Bad weather **plagued** the offensive, as the trenches filled with water and the field turned to mud. However, by September 16, Saint-Mihiel and the surrounding area were free of German occupation. The American forces shifted south to a new offensive near the Argonne Forest and Meuse River. There, they teamed up with British and French forces to crush the Germans.

Hundred Day Offensive

In early 1918, events still seemed grim for the Allied forces. Germany had launched a series of offensives that knocked back the Allied lines to within 43 miles (69 km) of Paris. But these actions proved to be Germany's final efforts. While German troops and resources were stretched even more, the Allies were receiving reinforcements and actually increasing their numbers. The Canadian Corps played a large part in these Allied offensives. The Canadian Corps gained a reputation for leading successful charges.

In August 1918, Allied leaders planned a major offensive in France. Canadian troops moved north to Ypres and tricked the Germans into thinking a major offensive was coming from that direction. The Canadian forces then secretly returned to the Amiens battlefront for the real attack. The Allies did not use artillery bombardment this time to surprise the Germans. The Canadian and Allied push resulted in an advance of almost 12 miles (19 km) in three days.

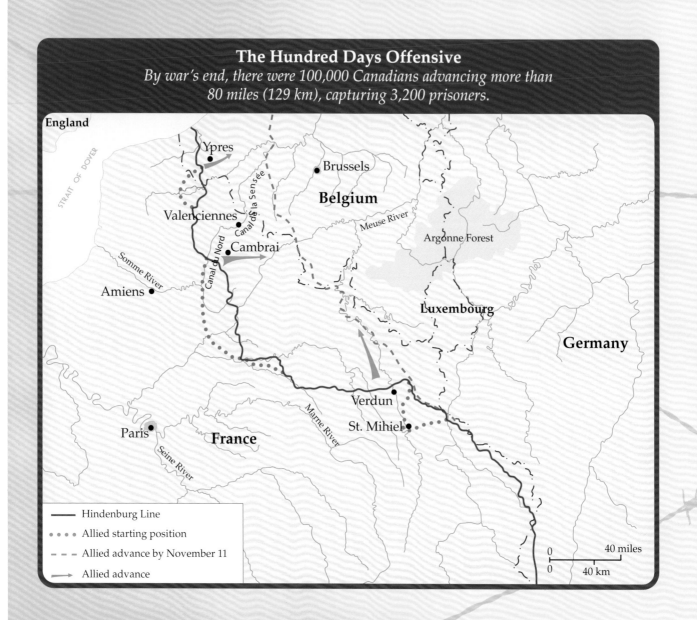

The Hundred Days Offensive
By war's end, there were 100,000 Canadians advancing more than 80 miles (129 km), capturing 3,200 prisoners.

England

Ypres

Brussels

Belgium

STRAIT OF DOVER

Canal de la Sensée

Valenciennes

Meuse River

Canal du Nord

Cambrai

Argonne Forest

Somme River

Amiens

Luxembourg

Germany

Verdun

Marne River

St. Mihiel

Paris

France

Seine River

—— Hindenburg Line

• • • • Allied starting position

– – – Allied advance by November 11

→ Allied advance

0   40 miles
0   40 km

CANADA'S HUNDRED DAYS

Because of the major role played by Canadian forces, the Hundred Day Offensive is often called Canada's Hundred Days. Fighting began in August 1918 and lasted until November 11, the day the armistice was signed.

ABOVE: *General Arthur Currie looks at the German guns captured at Amiens during the Hundred Days Offensive.*

The success of the push hurt the morale of the German troops as much as it boosted the morale of the Allies. The Allied forces next turned their attention to breaking the Hindenburg Line. Canadian troops moved to the Arras sector. After a week of intense fighting, the Canadian Corps broke the Drocourt-Quéant Line on September 2. Attention then turned to the Canal du Nord, which comprised part of the Hindenburg Line.

Canadian Corps Commander Lieutenant-General Arthur Currie had a plan. His troops would make their way across a 2,700-yard-wide (2,469 m) dry section of the canal. They would be joined by British troops. A narrow approach would cause troops and equipment to bunch up. To cover the advance, Currie called for the heaviest single-day bombardment of the entire war. Currie's plan led to success in the September 27 attack. The Canadians continued to help capture Cambrai. By October 11, the Canadian Corps had reached Canal de la Sensée. After that, they were sent to help capture Mont Houy and Valenciennes in early November. As the Allies pushed forward, the German army was beginning to crumble.

GERMANY REVOLTS

The Allies' massive assault on the Hindenburg Line destroyed the German army's last defensive position. The war was going badly for Germany, as were events at home. The Allies were calling for **Kaiser** Wilhelm II to step down and hand power to one of his grandsons. The kaiser refused but wanted an armistice nonetheless. This development discouraged the soldiers in the field.

The Greatest Moment in History

Exclusive Photographs by HELEN JOHNS KIRTLAND *and* LUCIAN SWIFT KIRTLAND, Leslie's Staff Correspondents

The signing of the Peace Treaty at Versailles on June 28th formally ended the greatest war in the history of the world, and as the German delegates attached their signatures the thoughts of many turned back to the days of 1871 when Bismarck imposed his stern conditions on the French delegates in the same hall.

First Two Pages of Peace Treaty Signatures

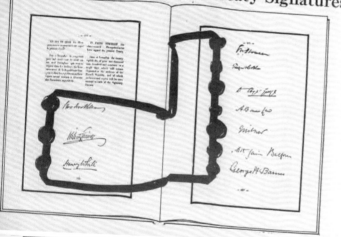

ABOVE: *The war came to an end on Monday, November 11, 1918, at 11 a..m.*

Austria-Hungary had surrendered on November 3. On November 7, Socialist party members in Bavaria led a revolt, declaring the overthrow of the German monarchy. Wilhelm II continued to resist, but he had lost control. His **abdication** was announced, against his will. He fled to Netherlands on November 10.

THE TREATY OF VERSAILLES

At five o'clock on the morning of November 11, 1918, a group of high-ranking German diplomats and military officers entered a railway car in the Forest of Compiègne. There, they met with representatives of the Allied forces to begin peace talks. Three weeks earlier, the German government had contacted U.S. President Woodrow Wilson. Germany asked that steps be taken to arrange an armistice. The Treaty of Versailles was signed on June 28, 1919. The Great War was officially over.

Many of the terms of the treaty punished Germany for its role in World War I. Germany lost 12 percent of its territory and about a tenth of its population. The boundaries of Poland were redrawn. Poland received part of what had been German **West Prussia** and a strip of territory on the Baltic Sea. The nation of Austria-Hungary was dissolved. Austria and Hungary became two separate nations. Some of its **constituents** received their independence. The Balkan states were re-formed as the Kingdom of Serbs, Croats, and Slovenes. Britain, France, Japan, and other Allied nations took over Germany's colonies in China, the Pacific, and Africa. Germany was ordered to sign a war guilt clause. It was forced to take responsibility for starting the war and to pay for damages suffered by Allied nations. For its war debt, Germany received a bill for 266 gold marks, equal to roughly $63 billion in U.S. dollars. The debt was later reduced to $33 billion. Today, that would be about $402 billion.

WHAT DO YOU THINK?
Do you think that the terms of the Treaty of Versailles were fair? Why or why not?

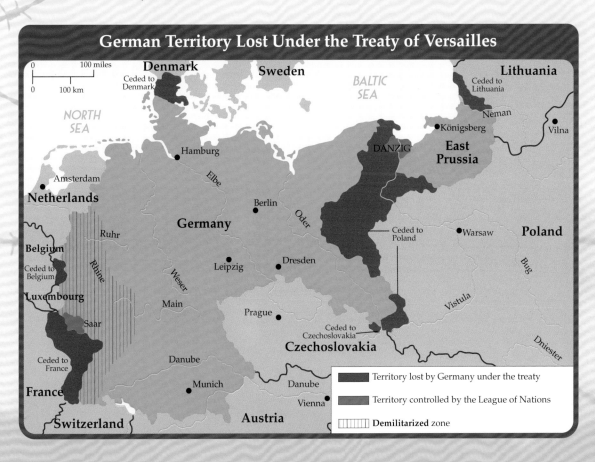

German Territory Lost Under the Treaty of Versailles

0   100 miles
0   100 km

Denmark
Ceded to Denmark
Sweden
BALTIC SEA
Lithuania
Ceded to Lithuania

NORTH SEA
Neman
Königsberg
Vilna

Hamburg
DANZIG
East Prussia

Amsterdam
Elbe
Netherlands
Berlin
Oder
Germany
Ceded to Poland
Warsaw
Poland

Ruhr
Belgium
Ceded to Belgium
Rhine
Leipzig
Dresden
Bug

Luxembourg
Weser
Main
Vistula

Saar
Prague
Ceded to Czechoslovakia
Dniester

Ceded to France
Danube
Czechoslovakia

France
Munich
Danube
Vienna
Territory lost by Germany under the treaty

Switzerland
Austria
Territory controlled by the League of Nations

Demilitarized zone

43

ABOVE: *This French cemetery at Verdun, France, commemorates those who fought and died in World War I.*

World War I changed the way the world looked to nations on both sides. Four major empires came to an end: Germany, Austria-Hungary, Russia, and the Ottoman Empire. War debts had a major effect on economies throughout Europe and the world, as well. As a result, **inflation** was out of control in many countries. While many breakthroughs in technology occurred during the war, changes also came for the status of women. Women had taken over many jobs and businesses while a large portion of the male population was away from home. Many women were not ready to give up those new freedoms when the men returned. Sadly, though, many men did not return. It is estimated that there were over 37 million total casualties in the war. More than half of those were on the Allied side. With such a huge blow to the population of young men, the number of women who did not marry or bear children increased significantly in the years following. Perhaps above all else, the world gained a new view of war after it was all over. The soldiers that did come home were often still suffering from shock. They brought with them accounts of the true horrors of modern warfare.

FURTHER READING AND WEBSITES

FURTHER READING

Adams, Simon. *DK Eyewitness Books: World War I*. New York: DK Publishing, 2007.

Audoin-Rouzeau, Stéphane and Annette Becker. *14–18: Understanding the Great War*. New York: Hill and Wang, 2002.

Baldwin, Hanson W. *World War I: An Outline History*. New York: Harper & Row Publishers, 1962.

Hart, Peter. *The Great War: A Combat History of the First World War*. New York: Oxford University Press, 2013.

Marshall, S.L.A. *World War I*. New York: Mariner Books, 2001.

WEBSITES

History.com, World War I
www.history.com/topics/world-war-i

BBC: World War One
www.bbc.co.uk/ww1

firstworldwar.com: a multimedia history of world war one
www.firstworldwar.com/

GLOSSARY

abdication	to formally give up power or responsibility
aerials	balloons or blimps, usually used to scout enemy positions
armistice	an agreement to stop fighting a war
artillery	large, long-range weapons, such as cannons, that are operated by crews
attrition	the gradual defeat of an enemy through constant attacks or by preventing them from getting new supplies
battlefront	location where opponents meet in battle
Bolsheviks	members of the radical Marxist party that seized power in Russia
bombardment	an attack with bombs, explosive shells, or missiles
boundary	a border or limit
breach	a hole or a gap; to break through a wall or defensive position
brigade	a military unit made up of combat battalions, with supporting units and services
bunker	an underground fortification
civilians	people who are not in the military
combustible	easily set on fire
communism	a political system created by Karl Marx in which the government controls all property
constituents	a resident of a district represented by an elected official
counterattack	attack by a defending force against an attacking enemy force to regain lost ground
counterintelligence	the branch of an intelligence service charged with keeping sensitive information from an enemy to prevent sabotage
czar	a Russian king; one of the former emperors of Russia
demilitarized	prohibited from having military forces or installations
deserted	illegally ran away from military service
Duma	the principal legislative assembly in Russia from 1906 to 1917 and since 1993

expeditionary	an armed force organized for service in a foreign country
inflation	when money loses its value, causing the prices of goods and services to increase
intelligence	secret information, especially about an enemy
interrupter	a mechanism that allowed pilots to fire machine guns safely without damaging the airplane's propeller blades.
kaiser	any of the emperors of Austria (1806–1918) or of Germany (1871–1918)
leaves	breaks; free time from military duties
lines	arrangements or placements of military forces
morale	feelings of enthusiasm or willingness that a person or a group has about a job
mutiny	open rebellion against an authority, usually by military personnel against superior officers
periscopes	instruments that use lenses and mirrors to provide a view of the water's surface or around an object
plagued	caused trouble for, bothered, or annoyed
reserves	a large stock from which to resupply equipment or soldiers as necessary
retreated	moved back from an enemy attack
salient	a battlefield section that extends or juts out into enemy territory
scorched earth	a military policy calling for the destruction of livestock, crops, and buildings in an area of operations
sentiment	what people think or feel about an issue
shelling	the bombardment of an area or target by artillery
strategy	an action plan
suffrage	the right to vote
synchronized	caused two or more things to happen at the same time
torpedo	a cigar shaped underwater missile designed to explode on contact with or near a target
U-boats	German submarines, in particular those used in World War I and World War II; short for *Unterseebooten*
West Prussia	a region of Northern Europe near the Baltic Sea, controlled mainly by Germany
wingspan	the distance between the tips of the wings on an aircraft

INDEX